The REALity of Interpersonal Leadership

A Guide to Leading Authentically

The REALity of Interpersonal Leadership

A Guide to Leading Authentically

Janelle A. Jordan, DBA

Fresh Ink Group
Guntersville

The REALity of Interpersonal Leadership
A Guide to Leading Authentically

Fresh Ink Group
An Imprint of:
The Fresh Ink Group, LLC
1021 Blount Avenue #931
Guntersville, AL 35976
Email: info@FreshInkGroup.com
FreshInkGroup.com

Edition 1.0 2024

Edited by Maryam Nawaz
Cover art by Anik / FIG
Cover by Stephen Geez / FIG
Book design by Amit Dey / FIG
Associate publisher Beem Weeks / FIG

Cataloging-in-Publication Recommendations:
SEL027000 SELF-HELP / Personal Growth / Success
BUS041000 BUSINESS & ECONOMICS / Management
BUS096000 BUSINESS & ECONOMICS / Office Management

Library of Congress Control Number: 2024917839
ISBN-13: 978-1-964998-14-5 Softcover
ISBN-13: 978-1-964998-15-2 Hardcover
ISBN-13: 978-1-964998-16-9 Ebooks

Contents

This journal is dedicated to those who want to lead genuinely, authentically, and transparently. Be unapologetic for being you and challenging the traditional norms of leaders. I hope you consciously work towards being an effective leader of autonomous teams.

Acknowledgments

God continues to show up in my life, but more importantly, in the seasons when I tend to get in my own way. I allow complacency to settle, and then He swoops in to make things uncomfortable. This is His way of letting me know that certain spaces no longer serve me. I pray that I will always be able to hear His voice and move according to His plan for me. For that, I am forever grateful.

To my family and friends who have become my family, thank you for being my rock. I see you all, and I feel your love. I hope to give you all at least an ounce of what you have poured into me. Thank you for being my sounding board and shoulders in challenging me when I was content.

Finally, to my readers, supporters, and those who have led me along my journey. I use every experience as an opportunity to learn. I try to remove my own lenses and see things through the eyes of others, as I truly believe most people do things with good intentions. Thank you for all the challenges and lessons I learned and for aiding me in my journey.

"Put people and passions above everything else, and you'll never fail."

Pat Summitt, per Candace Parker

Preface

When you look at some people in management positions, it begs to ask the question, how? They seem to lack a connection with their team and are merely focusing on the bottom line. While metrics are important and the reason companies stay in business, the people in the organization are just as important as the indicators, which are not met without them. This is where the differentiation between managers and leaders is derived. Managers focus on the results; conversely, leaders focus on the people who achieve the results.

The dynamics of the workforce are changing and will continue to evolve. From remote to on-site work locations, to a multigenerational culture and an array of demographics, how you lead the organization is tailored to the needs of those on your team. The ability for people to find another job and make more money is more prevalent now, post-pandemic. Hence, retention is critical to thrive.

The role of a leader extends beyond the training received. It is tailored to the rapport and connection built with each individual. One must learn to survive through authenticity and transparency while setting clear expectations and deliverables. There are real-life examples, relatable analogies, and quotes to summarize in making topics relatable. With the melting pot of people in the workplace, the onus is on the leader to connect with their team.

This journal serves to help those truly interested in leading interpersonally, premised on reality and transparency. Each week, the topic will enable the leader to delve into their thoughts from the content and capture their *Leadership Thoughts* in the respective section, the charge they will take into the week in applying it in the *Weekly Charge* section, and takeaways or feedback received from their approach in the *Weekly Takeaways* portion. Feedback is essential in improving as a leader, and at times, you can gage it based on the demeanor of your team members. This journal will assist in your journey to the REALity of interpersonal leadership and leading authentically.

Resolutions

With the start of any new year or season in a person's life, one tends to be hard at work identifying their resolutions and whether they are SMART (Specific, Measurable, Attainable, Realistic, and Timely). From a professional standpoint, you could probably use some accountability. What better way than to select a mentor heading into your season of resolutions? Honestly, this applies to our personal lives as well.

I've had the pleasure of having one of my mentors guide me in my professional journey and become a friend. I was initially his direct report but was immediately drawn into his enthusiasm. He was well-experienced and had a depth of knowledge about the company, but he genuinely took an interest in what was best for me personally and professionally. He embodied traits similar to mine, but his passion for his family was one I easily related to.

Nonetheless, he held me accountable, challenged me when I wanted to stay in my feelings, and was calm when I wanted to be the storm. If you do nothing else in your season of resolving, find a mentor and someone to hold you accountable. "Amen corners" won't help evolve you as a person. Let's normalize accountability and growth!

Leadership Thoughts:

_____

_____

_____

_____

_____

Weekly Charge:

_____

_____

_____

_____

_____

Weekly Takeaways:

_____

_____

_____

_____

_____

Cultural Upbringings

One's cultural upbringing or background aids in one's worldly perceptions. This is coupled with personal and professional experiences playing a significant role in a person's journey. These experiences are deeply rooted in the notion of family. As we spend most of the day at work, our peers tend to become our work family.

From a familial standpoint, my father's side is large. Most of my holidays and family events were spent at my grandmother's house on Sunnyside in Orangeburg, South Carolina. Yet, we grew up in what is noted as "The Reservations." Neither were glamorous neighborhoods, and we had to be creative in many things we did. While they weren't the best neighborhoods, it was home. We had extended family that lived one house down from us, and we were "The Crew" growing up. While we didn't have everything growing up, we had what we needed and made do with what we had. This led to having to be creative at times. Hence, I feel this regulated my approach to solving problems, as a pebble won't stop me, and I'm still going to work to push the boulder out of the way.

How much do you know about your team's background in shaping their perceptions? Cultural upbringings mold who we are and how we approach various scenarios. It innately builds character traits that are embedded in familial environments. Here's to my family and time spent on Sunnyside and The Reservations, even to the times spent in Saint Mary's Projects on Jackson and Westchester Avenue in the Bronx. Celebrate your upbringing and how it molds your mindset professionally!

Leadership Thoughts:

Weekly Charge:

Weekly Takeaways:

Setting Goals

In full transparency, I tend to set goals for myself at the beginning of the week and do so with affirmations of how the week will go. As I work to manifest a great week, it doesn't always go as planned; nonetheless, I reflect at the end of the day on how it all went. Albeit these goals can be mental, physical, and/or professional. Getting outside to walk/jog on a beautiful day is both mental and physical.

As I went for a walk one day, I set a goal to get under 16' on my walk/jog. This may be a small feat for some but huge for me, considering the screws I have in both knees. On this day, I decided to go to the park from my house to switch up the scenery. The pavement on the trail is uneven and cracked, with roots breaking up the pavement. As I was in my zone pacing myself, thinking, and heading into my third mile about to finish up, I tripped and fell. You can laugh because I did! I could've stopped, but I finished what I set out to do.

No matter how rocky the road, get up and finish! Also, don't take yourself too seriously and laugh even at yourself. As cliché as the sayings go, they hold true in "it's not how you start, but how you finish," … "it's about the marathon, not the race," … "focus on the war, not the battle." It all sums up to this … Set Goals, Then Crush Them!

Leadership Thoughts:

_____

_____

_____

_____

_____

Weekly Charge:

_____

_____

_____

_____

_____

Weekly Takeaways:

_____

_____

_____

_____

_____

_____

Blurred Lines

I've had some discussions lately where conversations between leaders and their direct reports are intended and perceived differently. The leader intends the conversations to be a coaching moment, while the employee takes it as a generic message and is not directed at any opportunities they may have.

As Stephen Covey stated, "we judge ourselves by our intentions and others by their behavior." These two must act in parallel in a coaching relationship. I believe leaders bear the burden of ensuring the message is clear yet delivered with empathy. The opportunities must be clearly stated, expectations for deliverables set, and the information must be recited at the end of the conversation to obtain understanding. You must own the corrective action and seek clarity if needed as an employee.

These conversations are not easy, but there will be mutual respect. I heard before that facts do not change feelings, but feelings change how you perceive facts. As a leader, one should embody the balance of being transparent and empathetic.

Leadership Thoughts:

Weekly Charge:

Weekly Takeaways:

Open Door Policy

It's nice to hear your manager say they have an Open Door Policy. As a leader, it's the right thing to say ... but only if you genuinely mean it.

When leaders walk in, your day is not your own. Everyone's problems are now placed upon you on top of what you already have planned. The load is heavy! Nonetheless, be genuine if you adopt this policy and don't turn employees away and/or dismiss their comments or needs. This is a huge deterrent! By doing so, they'll never come to you again, and you'll appear hypocritical. Trust me, word will spread quickly!

If the timing isn't right, simply ask for time to discuss it later. Stop typing or texting, and ensure you give the proper attention. This does not go to say drop everything then and there. They can respect you wrapping up something, or you can ask them to give you a moment and then give them your attention.

Remember, feedback is a gift—you either use it or you don't. You at least want to unwrap, process, and decide how or if you will use it. Immediately, shutting someone leads to them shutting down.

Leadership Thoughts:

Weekly Charge:

Weekly Takeaways:

Silence is Acceptance (Maybe)

Plato coined the quote, "Your silence gives consent." This has been a professional struggle for me as my personality intervenes. Being quiet has never been my strong suit, so in the workplace, I speak up when I see something awry. Whether it is for parity for a minority demographic or just the right thing to do, don't let silence be acceptance.

Now, if someone goes the route of ignorance and is draining your energy, let them bask in it. Jay-Z said, "A wise man told me don't argue with fools. Cause people from a distance can't tell who is who." Their lone voice can sometimes bring awareness in questioning, "What are we even talking about?" Again, sometimes, let them be great! In this case, it's okay where silence is acceptance.

My sister told me something from my dad: focus on the war, not the battles. If it's minor and not detrimental to anything but your pride in being right, let it ride. A tactful response is acceptable if you can change even one person's perspective for equality or for merely keeping your peace of mind. Lead with discernment.

Leadership Thoughts:

_____

_____

_____

_____

_____

_____

Weekly Charge:

_____

_____

_____

_____

_____

_____

Weekly Takeaways:

_____

_____

_____

_____

_____

_____

Grace

We tend to think of the word grace at times in the religious or spiritual context, as well as keep it separate from our work lives. However, grace applies in all aspects. As a leader, extend yourself grace, as you won't always have the answers. It's fine not to always be on your A-game and need help. It's alright to take time to decompress and show yourself … Grace!

When I had the opportunity to go to the Netherlands for work, I was working but away from the daily norm and enjoyed the beautiful scenery. I needed that time to show myself grace, decompress, and regroup.

With the focus being on mental health lately, let's normalize the fact that it's okay not to be okay and show yourself some grace. Guess what? It's okay not to have it all together but to do the work of figuring it out. The gotcha is … work to figure it out! Don't assume someone will just forget their need for you and things will magically work out. Find yourself a therapist, your place of peace, or whatever means you choose. "Grow through what you go through." Just give yourself some grace!

Leadership Thoughts:

Weekly Charge:

Weekly Takeaways:

Managing Expectations

When you hold people to the same or higher expectations as you would demonstrate, and they let you down, you're left holding a bag of emotions full of disappointment and frustration. Meanwhile, they do their business as usual while sleeping well at night. Stop letting people live rent-free in your head! Meet people where they are and understand you won't always get what you give. Give your effort and time without expectation. If they prove they can give more, take the "W," calibrate, and adjust accordingly. If there's a mishap, articulate your feelings as you seek to understand effectively. Remember—Grace.

Expectations are reciprocal. Focus on managing the emotions that come with preset expectations of others. Don't allow anyone to have that much power to control your reactions, especially in a professional setting. We're at work, to work. If we become friends, that's a bonus. As a friend, we should have mutual respect and the jobs we hold. There must be respect for the expectations of work.

Leadership Thoughts:

_____
_____
_____
_____
_____
_____

Weekly Charge:

_____
_____
_____
_____
_____
_____

Weekly Takeaways:

_____
_____
_____
_____
_____
_____

Authenticity

How do you respond when asked to bring your authentic self to work? Do you stay true to your personality, morals, confidence, truth, and transparency? On the other hand, are organizations prepared for your authentic self? Companies seek diversity of thought and physical attributes, but are the leaders really prepared to hear it?

Rhetorical questions but intended to provoke thought. Know your audience, yet stay true to yourself regardless of those who take offense. As the old saying goes, "A hit dog will holler!" If the statement made is relevant, don't dismiss what's being said. Truly attempt to empathize with what's stated. As I know this could be misconstrued, I wouldn't recommend using the verbiage you use with people outside of work if it could be deemed inappropriate, in addition to being mindful of clothing. Again, know your audience.

Nonetheless, I will tell someone I'm like an acquired taste—I ain't for everybody. That's the reality of being your authentic self. Choose to be YOU every time without dimming the light your personality emanates, without compromising your values, and without fear of using your voice while others merely "go along, to get along." Authenticity over duplicity! May your dopeness offend someone just by walking into the room. Be YOU … Be Great!

Leadership Thoughts:

_____

_____

_____

_____

_____

Weekly Charge:

_____

_____

_____

_____

_____

_____

Weekly Takeaways:

_____

_____

_____

_____

_____

_____

Reciprocity

Yes, it is like the type Lauryn Hill was singing about. But seriously, people tend to use titles, roles, and other determined labels of superiority for justification for not reciprocating respect shown to them. I know I spoke of managing expectations previously, but now I'm talking to the people in the back! How do you establish reciprocal relationships where you're no longer making managing expectations your go-to approach?

Leaders, your position does not equate to exhibiting non-equitable behaviors to others. When seeking respect, honesty, dedication, and all the positive traits you can think of for your team, you should also demonstrate these traits. These traits are not only reserved for your manager or for those who can benefit you. This is a quid pro quo relationship, where one person does something and expects something to be given in return. RECIPROCITY. Your team just wants to ensure they are seen and met where they are, with respect. Behaviors of reciprocity should extend throughout organizational hierarchies, from the CEO to the person cleaning up.

Don't get caught up wanting people to treat you like you treat them, then become surprised when they do, and it's not in alignment with what you thought you were demonstrating. Self-awareness is vital to ensuring your team feels valued. A team directly reflects their leader, hence the need for reciprocity.

Leadership Thoughts:

Weekly Charge:

Weekly Takeaways:

T.E.A.M.

You've probably heard the acronym for T.E.A.M., Together Everyone Achieves More. However, is this concept truly embodied in the workplace or conveniently utilized to achieve a person's interests, possibly on behalf of their respective group?

A team is generally defined as a group of people forming one side in a competitive sport or those coming together to achieve a common goal. Thus, this is a mutual relationship of people where the expectation of success is reciprocated. There goes that reciprocity! One can't decide to be a team or use the term when it only benefits self. When on a team, you must step up to help others without being self-seeking. Why? The simple answer is that it helps the team!

Just because you wear the same uniform doesn't mean you're on the same team. That might've gone over some people's heads, so let me repeat it. Just because you wear the same uniform doesn't mean you're on the same team. Discernment is critical! It is essential to ensure you have an alignment of the right people to define your team. Focus on creating a culture of engagement, empowerment, and constructive challenge while respecting one another. Do the things that help your team even if it is a slight inconvenience for you if it gains you nothing, but you can use your gifts to help, and more importantly, if it's in your realm, OWN IT! Trust me, the team will appreciate you for it.

The team reflects its leader. If the leader lacks confidence, is unorganized, and is self-serving, the team will be reluctant to align and follow. Of special note, your personal team needs to be just as strong as your professional team. Your personal team should pour into you, and you into them, so you can show up to work in optimal form.

Leadership Thoughts:

Weekly Charge:

Weekly Takeaways:

ENERGY

As I entered a new decade of life, I reflected on energy and its importance. Energy is defined as the strength required for physical and mental sustainability. How do you maintain that energy for those around you if you don't have it to give?

When leading others, they will reflect the energy you exert. Your emotional capacity must be charged up to give positivity while absorbing the pull from those who require your guidance. Your emotional bank will reap a negative balance if you're not in a good space. You have to decide how you will give good energy and how you charge up to be able to offer more. Honestly, you won't have it some days, but fighting back to find your center is important.

One's energy should be contagious when one enters a room; however, it is only deemed positive if it uplifts and empowers those around you. In building your energy, you must decide, "I Choose Me." You can't give what you don't have. People say protect your peace; some think it's cliche. Nahhh! Protect your peace so you have the energy to give others. This is Big Energy! Be a Vibe! Choose to be the energy that positively alters the atmosphere in the room.

Leadership Thoughts:

Weekly Charge:

Weekly Takeaways:

Value

When you think about value, monetary is one of the first things that comes to mind. However, value can be attributed to time, experience, or anything deemed beneficial to someone. As you lead others, are you ensuring you respect the value of their time and expertise and the intangibles they bring to the team?

We are human and tend to get caught up in the process while losing focus of the people. It's the people who keep everything going. If leaders don't prioritize the value of those on their team, it will lead to failure. Don't get me wrong now; value absolutely relates to money. The time and experience a person brings to the table should be quantified appropriately through monetary compensation. After all, we don't go to work as a hobby.

As you look at someone's value, you must examine underneath the surface. Sometimes, what doesn't shine is truly a gem; it just might need a little polishing. Don't let cubic zirconia keep you from appreciating the true beauty in a diamond that just needs some polishing. As leaders, value your people's time, experience, and whatever they need that is reasonable to support. After all, it's the pressure that helps form the diamond. People have earned that, justifying the value of those gems.

Leadership Thoughts:

_____

_____

_____

_____

_____

Weekly Charge:

_____

_____

_____

_____

_____

Weekly Takeaways:

_____

_____

_____

_____

_____

Investment

In this sense, investment is not strictly monetary but a personal investment in oneself. We go to work to handle our daily expenses and build fiscal wealth; however, how are you investing daily in yourself?

Society and workplace expectations tend to place undue pressure on us regarding where we need to be in life. There are things like getting a degree/certification, getting another degree/certification, getting some training, gaining more experience, reaching this goal by this age, and so on. We take these targets and make goals for ourselves, and then what? Do they enable us to become more qualified with theoretical knowledge but not practical? These are all investments in yourself, but where do you define that you are enough? How do you pour into your stability and ability to perform and lead as people meet you where you are?

I'm here to remind you that you are enough! The investments you make in yourself are solely YOUR decision for personal gratification. Pour into yourself so that you can be there for others. Invest mentally, spiritually, and emotionally so you can lead in the same manner and not based on a script or practiced dialogue. Capitalize on the investment you make in yourself!

Leadership Thoughts:

Weekly Charge:

Weekly Takeaways:

Criticism

Criticism is normally given from either a constructive or destructive stance. It is solely based on a one-sided perception of a subjective occurrence. Furthermore, it can be solicited or not. As once noted, "If you live by the cheers, you'll die by the boos." Criticism comes with the territory.

Self-reflection is important to determine its applicability regardless of the intent or source. Don't immediately become guarded and build up the Great Wall of China. Evaluate if there is something you can do differently and adjust or take notes and compartmentalize it to determine if there's a theme building later. Overall, it will all hinge on your response to it.

Don't let criticism from others consume and eat at you. Denzel Washington purportedly stated, "You'll never be criticized by someone who is doing more than you. You'll always be criticized by someone doing less. Remember that." Unfortunately, sometimes people have ill-intent and give it to stall the potential they see in you and your impact. Continue to push through with your purpose of leading the pack!

Leadership Thoughts:

_____

_____

_____

_____

_____

_____

Weekly Charge:

_____

_____

_____

_____

_____

_____

Weekly Takeaways:

_____

_____

_____

_____

_____

_____

Presence is a Present

Have you witnessed someone naturally influence others just by entering a room? Are they able to pull on the strengths of others and get engagement where some people struggle for a response? Some take it as a motivation to want to be that type of leader. Well, imitation is the best form of flattery. Others take it negatively and are unable to respond properly, so they try to target this ability as a divisive behavior.

When someone has the ability to shift a person, a team, or a room, you should go hone in on that. "My presence is a present," per Kanye West. If you don't like it, maybe you should reference the other part of the lyric (I'll leave you to Google). No, but seriously, don't tear down others for their ability to captivate people. Appreciate the gifts they radiate unto others just by showing up. Learn and grow from them if you desire to do the same.

LeBron James is known for saying, "Nothing is given. Everything is earned." They worked for the respect of others; thus, you must put in the time to earn the same. He also recently stated, "The real question is, can I play this game without cheating? The day I can't give the game everything on the floor is when I'll be done." Don't cheat the game to get where you want to be while tearing down others in the process. If you must cheat, it probably no longer serves you. Put in the work that you want to exude. Be great!

Leadership Thoughts:

_____

_____

_____

_____

_____

Weekly Charge:

_____

_____

_____

_____

_____

_____

Weekly Takeaways:

_____

_____

_____

_____

_____

And the Oscar goes to...

How often have we sat back and looked at those who know the right things to say but don't actually do them? How often do we see those who emulate the poor leadership they've seen and thought it was effective? Or how often do people stand up for the title, offending others to make themselves look good, then have no clue what to do? The answer is way too often! They are merely portraying the role of a leader.

One of my direct reports told me early on in my career that they could make me look good or make me a star. This was an initial conversation to get to know one another, so I asked for an explanation. He said they normally have leaders tell them what to do and not listen to them, where they averaged over 20 years of experience. So, in other words, they can do exactly what I say, knowing it was wrong, and I would reap the consequences; hence, get the wrong kind of shine as a star. Or we could work together, and they would make me look good. I chose to look good because that was my leadership style.

Unfortunately, some leaders get caught auditioning and putting on a facade of someone else. As the phrase goes, "A leopard can't change its spots." The act will eventually end. Drake lyrically advised in his song Trophies, "And they don't have no award for that. S*** don't come with trophies. No envelopes to open. I just do it 'cause I'm 'sposed to." You will have to decide to be an authentic leader consciously.

This is just a note to all leaders: don't demonstrate the behaviors you hate to be on the receiving end of and lose sight of your purpose in leading and developing others. The former ways of leading with an iron fist are no longer prevalent and effective in getting results. Stop putting on for who you think people above you want to see. Be YOU! There's no need to act any longer!

Leadership Thoughts:

_____

_____

_____

_____

_____

_____

Weekly Charge:

_____

_____

_____

_____

_____

_____

Weekly Takeaways:

_____

_____

_____

_____

_____

_____

Celebrating the Wins ("Dubs")

The expectation for leaders, teams, and individuals in life is to evolve and be better than we were. We tend to focus on our shortcomings or L's more, and it deters us from recognizing the progress we've actually made. This isn't fair to all who are impacted, including ourselves.

J. Cole said in I'm Coming Home, "To appreciate the sun, you gotta know what rain is." You're going to take some L's, being the rain, to celebrate the dubs, being the sunshine. Additionally, someone stated, "When you can't find the sunshine, be the sunshine." The work you have put in has paid dividends, regardless of how minute they may seem. It's all incremental. You're further along today than you were yesterday, last week, last month, last year, five years ago, etc. Pat yourself on the back for the progress that has been made.

Clear steps for the L's: 1) Take it, 2) Digest or Eat it, and 3) Get back on your grind! Denial fuels the fire, and it only strengthens you. Thanks to everyone who contributed to your L, right, wrong, or indifferent. You don't have to entertain or block them on social media platforms. Just let them see you shine, Sunshine!

As my wise eldest nephew reminded me, the past is the past. You're out here thriving and better than where you were. You're in a better place. So, celebrate your dubs and pop your ish!

Dust yourself from the L's; they will happen, but don't let them prosper. Continue to celebrate the wins, and let's get this dub!

Leadership Thoughts:

Weekly Charge:

Weekly Takeaways:

What's the Secret Sauce?

Have you ever looked at an effective leader and wondered how they can be change agents and engage a team towards optimal performance? How do they gain traction with others, both those they have direct or no responsibility for, and do so consistently and without being a jerk? Why are people gravitating towards them? What's the secret sauce?

Think about a leader who inspires you. It may bring thoughts of someone who encouraged, empowers, motivates, influences, and other synonymous words. The "WOW" factor prompts you to follow their lead or practice what they exude. One should be humbled if they inspire someone and should not be taken for granted. Nipsey Hussle said, "It is important to not squander the opportunity. The highest human act is to inspire."

One of the most important things to remember about inspiring others is that you normally inspire someone when you don't even know you're doing it. That's it, that's the secret sauce! It is as unique to someone as their fingerprint. You can see things you want to replicate in your style and approach, but it will never be an exact replica of anyone else. This all goes back to authenticity and being who you are.

Find who inspires you and be an inspiration to others. I saw this quote, "Never too big to learn, or too blind to be inspired. Even big homies, got big homies." Keep working on the recipe for the secret sauce. It will only be specific to you!

Leadership Thoughts:

_____

_____

_____

_____

_____

Weekly Charge:

_____

_____

_____

_____

_____

_____

Weekly Takeaways:

_____

_____

_____

_____

_____

Part of a Rare Breed

Being part of a rare breed is characterized by people or things contrary to the norms. They are the leaders who step away from the status quo and become change agents or even advocate for minority representation. They are unicorns, someone amazing and a rare find.

Leaders are called to the challenge to aid in developing people and processes for continuous improvement. Do we really get different results and continuously improve if we are surrounded by those who look, think, and act like us? Recently, Becky Hammond, former WNBA player, current Head Coach of the Las Vegas Aces, and recent inductee into the Hall of Fame (HOF), acknowledged Coach Gregg Popovich, formerly of the San Antonio Spurs, in her HOF acceptance speech for taking a chance on a female coach in the league. He's the rare breed who did what someone had never done in the NBA. Coach Pop acknowledged her potential and who she was as a person and encouraged her along the way. The mere statement, "Just be you; you're going to be great," spoke volumes about her and her career. Coach Hammond can now radiate and inspire a new generation of players based on his simple act of being a rare breed and giving her a chance.

Align yourselves with those who challenge you and your processes. If your circle doesn't do this for you, you should probably adjust your circle. Someone might not fit your "mold" concept, and that is alright. Become comfortable being a rare breed or unicorn. You can change the trajectory of someone's life, which can empower a generation in the future.

Leadership Thoughts:

Weekly Charge:

Weekly Takeaways:

Polaroid Picture

When you take a picture with a Polaroid, now known as an Instax, you wait patiently for the image to develop and hope the outcome is what you expected. The image could be blurry, catch someone laughing unexpectedly, or be a perfect recollection of the moment. Yet, that's what it is: a moment or a memory created from several takes.

When you're leading others, you establish memories or moments in their life that require things to come to fruition in determining if it'll be a blur, an unexpected outcome, or a perfect image. Nonetheless, it's the development stage and building of anticipation of what's coming. Neither you nor they will know how it will evolve, but trust the outcome and establish memories.

Over the summer, there were several clips of Blue Ivy dancing on stage with her mother, Beyoncé, while on tour. Each time, she improved her performance and became more confident. While others critiqued her, she was probably her own worst critic; however, I give kudos to her for being able to dance in front of sold-out shows, perfect her craft, and build an everlasting memory with her mother. This was the evolution of her Polaroid picture as it developed. There were a couple of takes, but the picture is analogous to her progress over the summer, which evolved and created a lasting memory.

How will you aid others in developing their Polaroids? There will be several attempts at the perfect picture, but don't forget the development process along the way to get there, as it'll take time. This applies to oneself, as well. Eckhart Tolle noted, "Some changes look negative on the surface but you will soon realize that space is being created in your life for something new to emerge." Create memories or moments on the journey for others as well as yourself. Oh, and as Andre 3000 said in OutKast's song Hey Ya, "Shake it like a Polaroid picture."

Leadership Thoughts:

_____

_____

_____

_____

_____

Weekly Charge:

_____

_____

_____

_____

_____

Weekly Takeaways:

_____

_____

_____

_____

_____

What's Your Mindset?

Discipline is the word we know we must demonstrate to get what we desire. It's setting standards to achieve a goal without compromising because of external influences. Perseverance is another word that resonates with the diligence it takes to achieve a goal, regardless of the present barriers. When deciding to lead, it takes discipline for your team and yourself to achieve goals and become an autonomous, high-performing team.

Kobe Bryant, a basketball legend, is revered for the work ethic he demonstrated outside of actual NBA games. He didn't just lend to his talent; he dedicated himself to evolving his craft in the game of basketball and would be laser-focused on the mindset of "Mamba Mentality." His mindset was keyed to being his best version and challenging others to do the same. Kobe did this to the extent that others have spoken about him working out while others went on to do leisure activities. This mindset permitted mental tenacity to be prepared for several in-game scenarios.

It takes discipline to hone your craft and perseverance to fight the things that create obstacles on the journey. Don't let a pebble stop you from being an extraordinary leader, and engage the help of your team to move boulders. Extraordinary people do extraordinary things by having the foundational aspects of discipline and perseverance.

So, what's your mindset? Where's your Mamba Mentality? As cliché as it sounds, we all have the same 24 hours; it's up to you how you choose to spend it.

Leadership Thoughts:

Weekly Charge:

Weekly Takeaways:

Team Identity

When evaluating a team, its identity and structure must be in place. This is a fundamental concept for teams we are on professionally and leisurely. The team identity is oftentimes rooted in the characteristics of the leader. The personality and approach to solving problems are usually premised on how the team views the leader behaving or reacting.

At the core of any team is analyzing strengths and opportunities. Reflecting on my time as an assistant coach for my high school alma mater, I realized that we had to work on our identity and ensure everyone knew their role. We knew our strength wasn't necessarily in shooting the ball well but was achieved through ball movement and creating opportunities to take set shots, or shots when you have all body mechanics in order, leading to a better chance of scoring. We needed to be agile in our offense but even better defensively and prepared to prevent the opposition from scoring. Our defensive presence and speed were our strengths, and creating offense from these opportunities allowed us to be successful. While this scenario is tailored towards sports, it is prevalent in evaluating the core values of a team overall.

Professionally, how do you align your players to prevent obstacles from preventing you from attaining your goal? Is your team better in one facet and thus creates opportunities subsequently in another aspect? As a leader, do you exhibit emotional intelligence or situational leadership when responding to various "in-game" scenarios? Whether a coach or player, leader, or team member, words resonate with the team identity, such as EXECUTION, COMMUNICATION, TOGETHERNESS, HUSTLE, HEART, and GRIND. In essence, we evolve these things to form a HABIT and start to change our opportunities into our strengths to create the team identity.

Leadership Thoughts:

Weekly Charge:

Weekly Takeaways:

What's Your Strategy?

One of my favorite things to do as a kid was to get home from school and on Saturday mornings, sit on the living room floor, and watch cartoons. At that time, I enjoyed Tom and Jerry, and Looney Tunes characters such as Road Runner and Wile E. Coyote. As I grew older, it evolved into Rugrats, as well as Pinky and the Brain. Even as an adult, I catch some episodes of SpongeBob SquarePants (no judgment, please). Each of these shows focuses on strategy and attaining a goal.

Focusing on Road Runner and Wile E. Coyote, Coyote was determined to catch the Road Runner in countless episodes but failed every time. He would implement these elaborate plans and come close but could never quite achieve his goal. Was his thinking short-sighted? Was the Road Runner thinking ten steps ahead of him? Or could it merely have been that he was working hard at the wrong things and missing the target, combined with veering in someone else's lane?

As you lead others, your strategy sets you apart from merely being a manager to being a people's leader. You can spend numerous hours on a task and seemingly make no progress, or you can establish a forward-thinking mindset that creates an autonomous team that achieves goals. The efforts of each character in the cartoon series were noted as needed to determine a plan to achieve their respective goal. They all started with intent, but intent doesn't always yield results. As I quote, this is merely a "Short-sighted vision for a long-term dream."

Be strategic as you lead a team. Remember, its chess, not checkers. In the cartoon Pinky and the Brain, Pinky asked Brain every episode what they were doing tonight. He responded, "The same thing we do every night: try to take over the world!" It's your strategy; how you get it done is up to you.

Leadership Thoughts:

Weekly Charge:

Weekly Takeaways:

Ready, Set, ACTION!

When you hear "Ready, Set, Action," one would think of a television or movie set. This indicates to everyone around that filming is about to take place, so prepare yourselves accordingly to focus on the scene being filmed. This is analogous to dreams, our lives, and impacting the lives we touch.

Ready equates to preparation for a task. How prepared are you to map out your development and the development of others and execute the plan to work towards a goal? The set is to be in a specified place or position. Are you physically and mentally in the place or space you aspire to be? Additionally, how do we help others to get there? Action is putting things in motion to achieve the goal. Are you merely "spinning your wheels" and living in the "One day I'm going to" mindset? Are you empowering others to move out of this place?

In every show or movie, there's a climax where events shift. You might see a build towards triumph, some failure, and then triumph again. Moreover, the story could continue evolving into sequels like the Fast & Furious movie series. Seemingly never ending with several turns of events. This translates to life and the dreams we're living out. There will be bumps and bruises, but continue with the story and change the narrative. Never stop striving to be better than you were the day before. What you're living now is what you prepared for years prior. It was once a dream in a previous moment of time.

Dream out loud to make your vision a reality. Lead and influence others as they see your journey. As Morgan Scott Peck said, "Let your dreams be bigger than your fears and your actions louder than your words." Continue to "Grow through what you go through."

Leadership Thoughts:

Weekly Charge:

Weekly Takeaways:

OWNership

The word ownership can tend to point the mind towards tangibles immediately. These tangibles could be a home or some physical asset. Ultimately, you assume responsibility for this property, including upkeep and, hopefully, upgrades for a return on investment.

From a leadership standpoint, there are some intangibles such as accountability, development, and commitment you own or are responsible for regarding your respective team. Again, these are intangible tasks, as you do not own people as a leader.

Holding yourself and others accountable speaks volumes of who you are as a leader. This entails holding yourself accountable for performance, deliverables, and gaps. Ownership is exemplified by holding all team members accountable if consistency is demonstrated. Development tends to coincide with positive influences of accountability. Discipline is established and has residual effects, thus contributing towards evolving future leaders and individual contributors, as everyone isn't set to lead. Commitment then becomes part of the status quo. If the team sees your commitment to win, lose, or draw, they will align to help ensure success.

As a leader, you OWN the development plan for yourself and your team. You OWN the successes and the opportunities. You OWN the communication of expectations and deliverables. Overarching, you OWN righting the ship. If the ship goes down, no one is looking for the first mate, quartermaster, or even seaman. They are looking for direction from the Captain of the Ship (reference the Titanic movie). If your team members are underperforming, as a leader, you either decide whether they belong on the ship or take ownership of correcting any identified gaps.

This can potentially be a huge undertaking, but I generally start each task of change with "Eating the elephant one bite at a time." If you have responsibility for a team, simply put … OWN it! Your OWNership defines the team as merely staying afloat or elevating to an autonomous organization.

Leadership Thoughts:

Weekly Charge:

Weekly Takeaways:

It's Game Time, Baby

In sporting events, the head coach is normally off to the side to help organize the team. There are Assistant Coaches and Players, either the Point Guard or Quarterback, who are also an extension of the Head Coach helping with the plays. These are the Generals, so to speak. The Generals are sometimes more interactive than the actual Head Coach during games. The reason? The Head Coach is the strategic thinker and has prepared the team for various situations during the match. They either correct the course during the game as needed or adjust it for upcoming games.

As a leader, you are fundamentally the Head Coach of the team. At various intervals, try this out. Take a moment, sit in silence, and observe your team at different times during the day. Of course, don't be a weirdo doing it! This can occur as they sit at their desks working, discuss tasks with one another, embrace each other's stories of family and experiences, and, most importantly, how they respond in meetings and discussions with others. Are they empowered? Are they adjusting amid work challenges? Are they responding with action and calm but with passion when needed? Are they actively listening? Are they taking OWNership? Are they demonstrating the two-way transaction of being held accountable and holding others accountable? Are they genuine? These are just some checks for calibration but are helpful for an autonomous team.

If you often find yourself correcting during the game, you haven't prepared the team for in-game situations. Please don't take this as letting the team plunder to defeat while interacting with others. However, you must give them the strategic plan, vision, expectations, and culture you expect off to the side in practice or one-on-one meetings. Coach them on the side so you are prepared to observe and respond as needed. You can't prepare their response in every scenario, but you must motivate them to think methodically. I always use the example of tying your shoes. You can loop-swoop-pull, bunny ears, or even Velcro. Either way, just tie them!

As a leader, coach from the sidelines, sit in silence, observe, and adjust accordingly. In moving in silence, you'll see the game through a different lens when you're not calling the plays. Quoting Lil Wayne, "Real G's move in silence like lasagna."

Leadership Thoughts:

_____

_____

_____

_____

_____

Weekly Charge:

_____

_____

_____

_____

_____

Weekly Takeaways:

_____

_____

_____

_____

_____

R-E-S-P-E-C-T

R-E-S-P-E-C-T. Find out what it means to me. Yes, along the lines of what Otis Redding and Aretha Franklin sang about. No, but seriously. Respect is defined as a feeling of deep admiration for someone or something elicited by their abilities, qualities, or achievements. It should be mutual in the workplace, but this is not merely in formalities extended. This is respect pertaining to respecting one another in completing things when it may not benefit you and holding yourselves and others accountable.

Leaders, you must respect your team when help is needed. As the saying goes, respect is earned; however, it is not given solely based on title. Respect should be given for people's time, ability to get things done, and dependency that someone regarded you highly enough that you wouldn't disappoint them. Mutual respect is also having uncomfortable conversations. If you respect the team enough to have lighthearted conversations, have enough respect to have those tough conversations to course correct.

It's a brief story of mutual respect. Someone on my team struggled to get to work on time. I respected this person and their abilities; nonetheless, I had to hold them to the same standards as others. Accordingly, I had to begin the disciplinary process. That person came back to me and thanked me over the weekend. They said they respected me for doing that and didn't want to disappoint me. This was only based on mutual respect and accountability. When you fail to fulfill an expectation, respect is lost with a dash of trust. Don't get me wrong, we all fall short at times and can't always meet everyone's needs, but it should be communicated and should not be a repetitive theme.

Leadership Thoughts:

_____

_____

_____

_____

_____

_____

Weekly Charge:

_____

_____

_____

_____

_____

_____

Weekly Takeaways:

_____

_____

_____

_____

_____

_____

_____

Can you hear me now? Good!

Does anyone remember the Verizon Wireless commercials where they asked, "Can you hear me now?" Followed by an enthusiastic "Good!" That commercial intended to demonstrate clarity and quality of their service, regardless of the setting, through propaganda; moreover, it conveyed clarity in communication, which consumers were seeking.

When you're sitting in the seat of a leader, are you listening or merely hearing what is being said? Some might argue there is no distinction, but many beg to differ. Hearing is the audible capability to perceive sound. Listening involves hearing and comprehending what is being said, processing it, and deciding to modify a behavior or action. Leaders, are you listening to respond to content or listening to respond to context? Don't let that go over your head!

As you build this skill, which may seem menial to some but is essential to being an effective leader, do so with intention. Be intentional with letting others know you are not listening to respond but listening to act. Don't just hear when others are talking, but instead actively listen. This reaps significant rewards as it opens the channels for receptivity, engages dialogue amongst the team, promotes an environment of creative thinking, and, more importantly, cultivates empowerment.

The campaign mentioned above ran most of the time with Verizon and later with Sprint to show clarity, reliability, and growth. As a leader, are you building clarity, reliability, and growth in your communication? Do you have a checks and balances system in place to meter for this with a simple "Can you hear me now?" Are you waiting for others to respond with, "Good!" or assuming there is clarity and quality? If not, possibly switch the proverbial "company," so to speak, in this case, approach, and adopt the Sprint twist with, "So I switched to Sprint, and millions more have, too. Can you hear that?" This is to check if the method of hearing or listening produces gains with others. It is the growth, as the switch will make all the difference.

Leadership Thoughts:

Weekly Charge:

Weekly Takeaways:

Much to Say, Little to Do

Have you ever been having a conversation where someone says, "All you gotta do is…" with little or no action? That statement is a double-edged sword. On the one hand, that person appears knowledgeable and feels as if they are guiding action. On the other hand, those on the receiving end of this conversation are capturing what is being said but have also stopped listening, as their ability to think independently was just disengaged.

Leaders, how do you walk someone through a solution while engaging their creativity? Let's focus on these fundamental approaches.

1. It's always a good practice to ask, "What do you think?"
2. Actively listen and ensure you understand the situation.
3. Brainstorm the potential situation and visually observe the challenge, if possible.
4. Reiterate the discussion with takeaways and deliverables.

Ensure alignment where they feel empowered to act and supported in the path forward. Don't allow them to go away with your plan but lack your vision and have insecurities about its execution and a fear of failing. This also leads to the next failure point of micromanaging. As a leader, your oversight should be forward-thinking and strategy-oriented, not down in the weeds.

So, the next time you catch yourself leading to a solution with, "All you gotta do is…", show restraint and guide the discussion towards a place of coaching. Your solution just may not be the best solution. Or, if the statement is hard to resist, put your money where your mouth is and put your words into action. The act of doing is more receptive than the mere act of saying.

Leadership Thoughts:

_____

_____

_____

_____

_____

_____

Weekly Charge:

_____

_____

_____

_____

_____

_____

Weekly Takeaways:

_____

_____

_____

_____

_____

_____

Let's Not Beat Around the Bush

We've all had a time in our lives when things were going great. Then, suddenly, they're not! The easiest thing you can do is let it be and let things run their course, while this is also the worst thing. Yet, the hardest thing to do is communicate with someone that something isn't working from your perspective. While this is applicable personally, this focus is professional.

In times like this, one important thing to do is reflect on when the discourse started. You don't always have to agree with someone else's views, but you can respect their viewpoint. When you're leading, the ability to conduct these conversations is critical. You must dig to the root of the problem and face whatever criticism comes to you head-on. Then, you must be decisive if it is worth taking action or receiving what the other person is saying to evaluate further for applicability.

You'll often hear that the business world is cutthroat, and you must have tough skin. The focus on the tough skin part is only due to expecting that you must be prepared to not only deliver tough messages but receive them as well. Loyalty and respect are becoming part of lost art, only to be consumed by participation trophies and watered-down messages. If you laugh with someone and are comfortable with casual conversations, have the same comfort in discussing subjects where there might not be mutual alignment.

Some things to note in having hard conversations are as follows:

1. Prepare yourself to address the subject head-on while remaining open-minded to the other person's perspective.

2. Set the tone to ensure that what is intended to be conveyed is not misconstrued.

3. Stand firm in who you are! Be transparent and authentic, as you will have to own the result in the end. Don't compromise yourself for someone else's comfort.

Leadership Thoughts:

_____

_____

_____

_____

_____

Weekly Charge:

_____

_____

_____

_____

_____

Weekly Takeaways:

_____

_____

_____

_____

_____

Validation Requirements

At certain times of the year we emerge into one of the favorite times with professional and collegiate football and basketball taking place. Fans are all dressed in their favorite team's apparel, cheering them on to a hopeful victory. All is well while your team is winning ... until it's not! Or when you "Decide to take your talents to South Beach."

Some of the most popular players have people who love or despise them. Whatever the reason, they're either the hero or the villain. Everyone will not always cheer for them, and that's okay. More importantly, if you have people who always agree with your actions and don't challenge you, are you genuinely improving?

When LeBron James decided to "take his talents to South Beach," Miami Heat fans were thrilled. In contrast, Cleveland Cavalier fans went as far as to burn his jersey. Their validation of his decision didn't matter; he did so to fulfill his dream. He later returned to fulfill the dream of Cleveland to win a championship. The same could be said of Deion Sanders in his move from Jackson State to Colorado. This was for exposure for his children. They were the same players they were at Jackson, but being in Colorado gave them the attention they deserved, although attending an HBCU (Historically Black Colleges and Universities). They hated Deion, and some cheered for him based on the results in Colorado.

All this to say, as a leader, you will do things that go against popular opinion. You will either be the hero or villain and don't require the validation of others. Just remember these key points:

1. Speak factually, and when you don't, put that disclaimer out there that it's your opinion.
2. Remain consistent and fair in your decisions. It'll be your standard, and people will respect you for decisions around the process, not specific people.
3. Be comfortable with making mistakes. Speak rationally about the choice being made, own the result, and adjust accordingly, if needed.

Everyone won't be rooting for you, and that's okay. Root for your damn self! Self-validation is all that is required.

Leadership Thoughts:

Weekly Charge:

Weekly Takeaways:

Purpose

When you define purpose, it usually resonates with existence and being. It is an intangible thing that can serve as a compass in our path of life. It leads to who we are and the reason or season we are placed in environments or situations.

As a leader, part of your purpose is to help shape the path of those you lead. It is to help them identify and walk proudly in their purpose. Challenge their norms, help them delve deeper into their desires, and watch their evolution. This will not happen in every facet, only in those where people are open to possibilities and growth. This is a reciprocal relationship.

Purpose is an ever-evolving cycle. One of my favorite quotes by Ralph Waldo Emerson is, "Do not go where the path may lead, go instead where there is no path and leave a trail." What you do in charting your path as a leader is, in part, fulfilling your purpose and aiding in the development of others. Help them envision possibilities that are unthinkable and walk paths unseen.

May you live in your purpose while helping others find theirs. The results won't be immediate, but the journey is rewarding.

Leadership Thoughts:

Weekly Charge:

Weekly Takeaways:

Journey Not the Destination

Children are generally asked what they want to be when they grow up. The response is typically filled with excitement, ambition, hope, and promise. There's no care in the world, just the attainment of the goal as they eagerly give a response.

Then, reality sets in, and children transition into pre-teenagers, teenagers, young adults, and adults. During this transformation, it is realized early on that things don't necessarily go as planned. The road is filled with twists and turns, the plot thickens, or the vision possibly changes. Nonetheless, each obstacle encountered contributes to the development of character. The journey, not the destination, encompasses who we are and what we contribute as leaders.

Adversity is guaranteed to present itself, but it's all in how you respond. It will help develop character and put you exactly where you're supposed to be. As a leader, your team watches you and how you handle adversity. Do you panic? Do you fold? Or do you hold it together to remove the obstacle? That's what life prepares us for: to lead and remove obstacles. It's all in your response to challenges, but use discernment with those around you. See who is serving the purpose but may need to guide them and pull them along, as well as those who may need to "get off the bus."

Don't let a pebble stop you. Jump over it and let your team help you push the boulder out of the way!

Leadership Thoughts:

Weekly Charge:

Weekly Takeaways:

I'm Emotional

Carl Thomas wrote a song titled Emotional. In it, he states, "I'm emotional, and I can't let go … I am trying to hold on to you." As a leader, it is vital to release the emotion from the decisions we make. Otherwise, it won't serve the organization's purpose but our selfish agendas. Don't confuse the emotions you have with the facts. Some state in varying ways that facts may change feelings, but feelings won't change facts. Don't make an emotional decision that impedes the overall goal.

The terms emotional and leadership rarely exist in the same exchange. Historically, leaders were not as empathetic to others and were primarily focused on work. As generations in the workforce transitioned, so did the introduction of acknowledging emotions of yourself and those you lead. Organizations are focused more on soft skills for their leaders for engagement and retention. However, where is the line between being emotional when leading and making decisions?

As a leader, you are responsible for guiding and developing others. Albeit a manager, educator, or coach, you hold the future of others in your hands, and it shouldn't be taken for granted. Focus on the facts and where development is needed. Avoid being reactive and living in the moment; contrariwise, think proactively towards the future. Foster the training model of 70-20-10. This is where 70% of knowledge comes from practical professional experiences, 20% from working alongside others, and 10% from theoretical knowledge and training. Guide others towards the 20% and 10% so they can chart their path of 70% to solve problems. Advocate their ability to learn and grow in gaining situational awareness. Learnings, or miscues, will happen. It is the response that contributes to the 70%. Avoid demoralizing someone from a misstep by coaching them through alternatives. Otherwise, you can hinder their engagement, lead to micromanagement, and promote fear of being penalized when being autonomous.

When leading others, the only acceptable emotion for decisions is emotional intelligence. This is premised on balancing self-awareness, empathy, motivation, self-regulation, and social skills. As a leader, how do you control your emotions while understanding the emotions of those around you?

Leadership Thoughts:

Weekly Charge:

Weekly Takeaways:

Collaboration

A collaboration is when two or more parties work together to achieve an end goal. We see the efforts of collaborations in various sectors, such as music, and in the workplace while leading teams and working with cross-functional groups.

In the music industry, collaborations are referenced as "collabs," where artists combine their creativity to form a song. This art form is appreciated when the musicians resonate with Erykah Badu in her song Tyrone, stating, "Now keep in mind that I'm an artist, and I'm sensitive about my ish." But seriously, each artist brings their own unique styles and melodies, and they flow to a song to bring about some of your favorite tunes. It is their ability to work together to form a masterpiece.

In professional settings, "collabs" can benefit the organizational goals of corporations, academia, and numerous other organizations. In these collaborative efforts, as a leader, you must convey the organizational vision to your team while keeping the overarching mission in mind to your end-user. The ability to do so is conceptually centered around teamwork with communication, clear expectations, deliverables, and accountability. It is the agility in handling not only dynamic environments but relationships as well. There is not a "cookie cutter" approach to leading. It is your unique staple, allowing you to interact and guide vertically and horizontally.

Some of my favorite, but not all-inclusive "collabs" are On My Own by Patti LaBelle featuring Michael McDonald, Run-DMC featuring Aerosmith in Walk This Way, Fire and Desire by Rick James and Teena Marie; All of the Lights by Kanye West featuring Kid Audi and Rihanna; and Run This Town by JAY-Z, Rihanna, and Kanye West. This is based on preference and some bias, but they all include artists from different or similar genres, varying styles, and differing backgrounds of the artists to create music catered to a respective audience or audiences.

This is akin to leading teams with people of differing backgrounds, ethnicities, and expertise to power the organizational engine. This type of collaboration serves a dual in feeding people's growth and customer needs.

Leadership Thoughts:

Weekly Charge:

Weekly Takeaways:

Chasing Significance
Over Success

As we work to find our purpose, we must ensure we know where it is grounded. As a leader, is it in success or significance? Can you achieve success to gain significance, or can you achieve significance to attain success?

Success can be measured in many aspects. Success can be defined as achieving a goal, serving a purpose, financial gain, or position. These are all indicators of achievement, and we then tend to set another goal after its attainment or feel defeated when it's not. Success tends to align with a personal focus, while it can also include a team goal if extended with that mindset.

Significance, on the other hand, is more applicable to value or worth. This can be viewed in what we pour into others as leaders. The extension of significance helps others to grow and develop. While you may not always have something personal to account for or receive, seeing those you lead evolve is rewarding in and of itself. It is the success, so to speak, achieved from the worth you bring and its impact on others.

So, which is it, significance or success? This question was posed to me, and the answer is simple yet multifaceted. My initial reaction was significance, as I always wanted to add value and fuel my purpose as a servant leader. Even if you've impacted at least one person, you are significant. Then I wondered, does this ultimately lead to success if it is part of your passion or purpose? Purpose can be grounded in significance over success. However, as leaders, the process steers more so toward the impact of lives touched and not merely captured in titles.

Significance, success, or both? Where do you find the most value as a leader, and which impacts those you lead more if you serve your purpose?

Leadership Thoughts:

Weekly Charge:

Weekly Takeaways:

Humility... The Gift and
The Curse

When we hear the word humility, one tends to think of meekness or not boasting of one's accomplishments or capabilities. It is a descriptive word for modesty, holding oneself in a lower regard while recognizing the importance of others. Yet, why does this word leave the interpretation either on the side of insecurity or arrogance? What's the gift and the curse of humility in leading others?

In Kendrick Lamar's song, Humble, his lyrical play speaks of working his way from the bottom to the top, being authentic, demonstrating humility, and basking in confidence. Kendrick spoke of authenticity, saying, "I'm so sick and tired of Photoshop." This is coupled with trials to triumph with, "I remember syrup sandwiches and crime allowances," to "This that Grey Poupon, that Evian, that TED Talk." Why keep completely quiet when your leadership story is to guide and inspire others? When you sit in rooms where you can influence the conversation, are you merely sitting idly by or presenting a differing perspective that may counter the popular opinion?

Conversely, triumph should be a testimony while not meaning to put off others. The focus is the journey, not merely the destination. The destination can be a moving target; each phase will enhance your identity. Those you lead don't want to hear where you are now, as it is evident in your role. Instead, help them elevate and reach their potential where they have their own story of humility.

Humility is analogous in a variety of situations. It's like walking a tightrope and maintaining your balance to ensure you don't fall off. One misstep can lead to a fall on either side. Or akin to headlights on a car. Dimming your light can prevent you from clearly seeing your way; however, caution on-comers when using your high beams and blinding others. It's the gift and curse of it all. If you do not have enough humility, you seem arrogant, while exhibiting too much, and you could appear weak. Find your humility in your E.G.O., Exuding Greatness Only!

Leadership Thoughts:

_____

_____

_____

_____

_____

_____

Weekly Charge:

_____

_____

_____

_____

_____

_____

Weekly Takeaways:

_____

_____

_____

_____

_____

_____

Fear Over Regret

When you think of the words fear and regret, one may wonder if they are discrete or causal. Does the fear or being afraid to take on a task merely stop there, or is the existence of the "what if's" from regret left lingering? Does the regret from prior disappointments yield fear of taking another chance? Are they two sides of the same coin?

When you lead others, you will live in an array of emotions in which emotional intelligence, or EQ, and situational awareness will be vital in choosing a path. Your team and peers will be observing how you respond. You must be decisive and own the path forward if the choice is based on data, logic, and situational awareness. The most important part of this is OWN IT! You must be able to speak to it and not live with fear in the land of the "what ifs."

Once a choice is made, regret might have a residual effect. However, regret doesn't have to be the final stop. You can embrace fear in an uncomfortable space and choose to chart forward toward your purpose. The lasting, negative implications of regret are only controlled if you decide to stay there. Instead, let fear propel you beyond complacency and comforts of the norms. Create new norms!

Leaders, chart your path of fear over regret. You will either see the other side of success or opportunity. The only positive of regret is ensuring you don't repeat past behaviors if presented with a specific situation again. It will only enhance your leadership adeptness over time.

Leadership Thoughts:

_____

_____

_____

_____

_____

_____

Weekly Charge:

_____

_____

_____

_____

_____

_____

Weekly Takeaways:

_____

_____

_____

_____

_____

_____

EXCELlence

The root word in excellence is excel. When one excels at something, they have achieved a level of competency that equates or surpasses a task or subject matter. It is truly believed that no one undertakes a task intending to fail or be subpar. As an unknown auther noted, "Strive for excellence, not perfection: Excellence allows you to accept mistakes and lean from them, while perfection doesn't.." So how do we merge intentions into deliberate behavior, yielding EXCELlence?

In the realm of leadership, the ability to excel is not merely constrained to the individual leader. EXCELlence is achieved by leveraging the strengths of each team member to achieve the ultimate goal. Think of the many sports that require each person's skillsets in their respective role. That is how you achieve the win and collectively excel as a team.

In charting the path to EXCELlence, scribe the journey for yourself and your team. Plan out the mission, vision, and purpose and determine the path. Without these things, there would be aimless wandering. The plan enables accountability and the ability to see your thought process from a certain time, re-evaluate, and plan your next thoughts. Complacency is a pretense of your success. Continue the quest to EXCELlence!

Leadership Thoughts:

_____

_____

_____

_____

_____

Weekly Charge:

_____

_____

_____

_____

_____

Weekly Takeaways:

_____

_____

_____

_____

_____

kNOw It All

The common comparison of confidence versus arrogance still rings true. When sitting back and observing someone exude a certain level of assurance, aptitude, and authenticity, do you construe it as arrogance or confidence? Is their demeanor premised on validation or previous experiences driving the approach? When attempting to place a label definitively, is it coupled with a person's sense of being or the recipient's perspective?

These two meanings can be blurred based on the eye of the beholder. Being competent and able to demonstrate these capabilities instills a level of confidence. Yet, some perceive this as a means to boast and stand out amongst others. With being a competent leader, the lines could potentially be straddled. Otherwise, one might be perceived as too meek or too cocky.

When others look to follow you, they want to ensure they follow a confident leader, or trust doesn't exist. Without trust, your team will undermine you and will be unsure of the vision you have for the team and their development. Likewise, this is essential in working alongside peers and upper levels of leadership. In this instance, you would still need confidence, but the sense of belonging, sometimes viewed as arrogance, should be considered a viable approach that allows you to sit at the table.

Ultimately, in the debate, the label of confident or arrogant can be oblivious to the person but glaring at the audience. It is up to you to measure the temperament of those you lead, work alongside, and are subordinate to and whether or not you are leaning heavily on one side versus the other.

Leadership Thoughts:

Weekly Charge:

Weekly Takeaways:

Peeling Back the Layers

The saying "peeling back the layers" is metaphorically grounded in finding something deeper, getting the core of things, and finding something new. An onion is generally used in this instance as the outer layer of an onion could tend to discolor, indicating that it might not be fresh. However, as you peel back the layers, the realization of a viable substance appears. No, this is not about food; yet it is about getting into the premise of serving in the role of a manager.

Serving is purposefully used as a manager is in a position to serve the needs of its people and ensure organizational goals are met. Nevertheless, are people accepting the role of manager in title only? Is the rationale merely based on the pay incentive when becoming a manager? Does it pose a sense of superiority when acquiring the role? Current trends differentiate managers and leaders, with one focusing on sustaining a process while the other is premised on human capital.

So, let's "peel back the layers" of the true expectations of a leader. It should not be taken lightly when presented with the opportunity to become a people's leader. You are expected to set the strategy and develop talent, and crazy enough … you get paid to do it! If you only plan to earn a check and not have to aid your team's morale and emotional support, get out of the role! There are people actually counting on their manager to guide and develop them. Hence, the core of leadership and peeling back the layers … leading with the heart!

Leadership Thoughts:

Weekly Charge:

Weekly Takeaways:

It's the Warmup

When preparing to engage in an athletic activity, it is always suggested that you warm up properly with stretching. Stretching aids in mobility, agility, and the prevention of injuries. You do this to get your body ready for the activity ahead. Similarly, people lift weights to become stronger and engage their muscle memory to make doing so easier as time progresses. Some aches and soreness are associated with doing so, but over time, your body acclimatizes, and it becomes easier until you push the needle and set progressive goals.

As leaders, are we allowing "stretching" to occur within our team? Are we permitting stretch assignments, and possibly someone who doesn't check all the boxes, an opportunity to develop and evolve based on foundational attributes they bring? While one may not have the exact skill set, how would they otherwise acquire it if they could not do so? Furthermore, one of the hardest transitions is with someone with experience primarily in one function but KSA's (knowledge, skills, and abilities) that could apply in another. Don't limit your team's diversity of thought by not wanting to develop. They are referred to as stretch roles and assignments for a reason. You're warming up, stretching, and preparing so you will eventually be ready for the task at hand.

You are responsible for identifying talent for these stretch opportunities as a leader. Are you cultivating a space for this to take place? Are you giving others the same chance you want others to give you? So, in Kanye West's The New Workout Plan, take heed with "One, and two, and three, and four, and get them sit-ups right, and tuck yo' tummy tight and do yo' crunches like this." Not literally, but metaphorically as we motivate others, get the warmup and stretching done, and prepare them for the next role.

Leadership Thoughts:

Weekly Charge:

Weekly Takeaways:

Never TOO Much

As we reflect on the word too, it indicates that something or someone is above average and possibly exceeding standards. While connotatively, it can affirmatively describe one's character or behavior. Conversely, it sometimes garners an adverse impression when a limited perception deems someone too confident or aggressive. Why is this deemed negative when monotonous group thinking yields average or subpar results?

When you examine the traits you see in a leader, there are those of confidence, decisiveness, empowerment, strength of will, and persuasiveness. They are able to command the room without a title, but their mere presence enables mutual respect. While these are just some attributes, adding the seasoning of "too" tends to taint the leader's ability by those who are unable to garner such attributes or those who tend to demand respect by title.

As leaders, we should always look to perfect our craft and other methods to lead others. Leaders should put true effort into their craft to constantly evolve and remain competitive in an ever-changing environment. The critique of "too" should not be used to diminish others. Yet, it should examine varying aspects of leadership. Luther Vandross harmoniously sang, "Never too much, never too much, never too much." As a leader on the receiving end of the "too" label, please note those are others' limitations and boundaries. S.C. Laurie stated, "You will be too raw for some. You will be too loud, too big, too fierce, too quiet, too deep. These are not your people."

Leadership carries its own uniqueness and identity. As Dolly Parton is noted in saying, "Find out who you are, and do it on purpose." Don't wait or allow others to define your worth; go out there, set the bar, and demand your worth. Celebrate others "too" when you are a benefactor and when greatness is recognized. Be too confident, too transparent, too caring, and too strategic, but most importantly, be too much YOU!

Leadership Thoughts:

Weekly Charge:

Weekly Takeaways:

Can I Speak to a Representative, Please?

Okay, clear your mind and close in on a moment when you pitched an idea to your manager that wasn't well received. In fact, remember how you might've felt deflated but hopeful that they would truly put some consideration into your proposal. Then, suddenly, the same idea you pitched was later presented, with your manager being the "originator" of the concept. No credit is given to you; it is merely the expectation of you continuing to work—the frustration, anger, and disappointment accompanying that moment. Now fast forward with the tables turned and you being the leader. Are you ensuring you don't create the continuous cycle you endured?

Being a leader is a trusted responsibility. Think about all the effort, ingenuity, and perseverance given, only to not receive credit for your efforts. You may gain temporary success in merit; however, you lose the trust of those you lead. At that point, you are an automated system lacking empathy and emotional intelligence, leaving your team requesting to speak to a customer service representative. They are seeking some sort of interpersonal leadership and connection that goes beyond titles and promotions.

Greatness is a choice, and we get to make that decision daily. This pairs with authenticity as well. Rory Vaden stated, "Success is never owned; it's rented, and the rent is due daily." Payment is made with the currency of YOUR accomplishments, in addition to doing right by others. As a leader, you bear the burden of putting others first, developing them, and giving them the exposure and credit they have earned. Note that there is an emphasis on earning, as everyone isn't deserving.

When you put on your leadership hat and reflect, think about the integrity, ethics, and moral responsibilities that come with it. In the end, ask yourself if you would be comfortable managing someone like you. Do you reflect on the qualities you wish someone had given you if you were just given a chance? Be the change you want to see.

Leadership Thoughts:

Weekly Charge:

Weekly Takeaways:

Not For Public Viewing

Have you ever seen a post where someone does a good deed, and it immediately becomes distasteful as they exploit the person or situation for "likes" on social media? Did you just wonder, do your good deed but aid in the person's dignity you're helping by not posting them unless there was going to be a benefit for the person in need? Well, functioning as a leader is akin to this situation.

Leadership permits the opportunity to set the vision for your team, create a healthy environment that promotes innovation, and foster empowerment in developing your team. Not doing so diminishes the leader's trust and emits an "I" atmosphere that discourages collaboration, where the leader takes credit for resolving an issue or coaching someone to work through a situation. Using the analogy of raising a child, you show them how to act and speak at home so they are well-mannered and do the right things in public. You don't openly take credit as a parent when they implement what they've been taught. You sit back, observantly quiet, and bask in the fact that you are raising a good human being.

Wanting to be acknowledged for the work you've put into growing others can be innate; nevertheless, there is a means to do so when your team members are recognized or even promoted to increasing roles of responsibility. This is how a natural mentoring relationship begins and extends well beyond hierarchical structures. The need for everyone to see what you're doing can leave you on an island alone as your team no longer feels empowered and leaves you with a potential dictatorial team.

So, when things are going right for someone on your team, and they're knocking it out of the park, ask them, "How can I support you?" Continue to encourage them, clap for them, and most importantly, pour into them. They'll give you credit for their development, and there'll be no need for "likes."

Leadership Thoughts:

Weekly Charge:

Weekly Takeaways:

Underdog

Everyone loves a good underdog story, right? Think of some of the greatest underdog triumphs of all time. There's David versus Goliath, Rudy of Notre Dame, The Karate Kid, Rocky, and later Creed, and numerous sports teams or athletes competing amongst the greats who prevailed victoriously. The underdog is not expected to win, with all odds are against them. Nonetheless, their intrinsic motivation and the few people cheering them on lead them to victory.

You may ask how this is prevalent in leadership. How often have you seen people get a job when others thought the veteran employee would? Or how many times were the odds pitted against you personally? When you take on a leadership position, it's not always the intangibles that get you noticed. The tangibles, such as key performance indicators (KPIs), where you must stand out amongst the best of the best.

Being "the new kid on the block" through internal promotions or external onboarding presents its own challenges. You may even be the recipient of the team with the most opportunity. However, this is where you shine! This is where the underdog prevails!

There are three basic rules when taking on a team:

1. Observe - Determine what the metrics are and your team's baseline. Evaluate the trends for the past three months, then where the team was a year ago. There's no need to reinvent the wheel. See what's working for those groups who are meeting the mark or the best practices, and align the team accordingly.

2. Bench strength - Hold one-on-ones with your team to get their perception of the team, the strengths and opportunities, and career aspirations. Preferably, have them prepare a SWOT (Strengths, Weaknesses, Opportunities, and Threats) analysis for themselves and the team beforehand. This will enable you to start working on the chess pieces.

3. Goal setting - It's been said, "Eat the elephant one bite at a time." The goals and vision set for the team must be step goals, meaning they are realistic and attainable. Once achieved, move the mark higher. Otherwise, the team won't attempt the hefty goal as they'll feel they can't attain it. Furthermore, ensure expectations are properly communicated.

Leadership Thoughts:

Weekly Charge:

Weekly Takeaways:

Uncharted Territory

Stepping into a leadership role can be both an exciting and scary place. If you're new to it, you don't know quite what to expect; however, you've seen others whose leadership you admire and those who had opportunities in that arena. Nonetheless, there are some foundational aspects. For experienced leaders, obtaining a new role is similar to a new leader. You may be unfamiliar with the players, but you must still put your trademark on shaping the team's identity.

This then becomes uncharted territory, but that's the beauty of it all. It is a blank canvas with guidelines, not rules, to guide your organization. Note that guidelines are your gray area for discretionary use. Meanwhile, rules are more rigid, and the company typically sets forth your ethics and other policies. On this blank slate, the standards are set by you in alignment with the organization's goals. Keep that in the forefront of charting a high-performing team.

Some basics in performing in the unknown are as follows:

1. Cultivate a safe environment where the members of the team feel heard.

2. Permit authenticity to take place as it then leads to innovation.

3. Be vulnerable with your team in open and personal spaces as we spend much time at work, and doing so helps bond and form relationships.

Anyone can manage with strong people they are familiar with, but it takes a leader to build a team up regardless of the organization. One must be able to lead in the trenches and triumph. Per Candace Parker, Pat Summitt is referenced as saying, "Put people and passions above everything else, and you'll never fail." The results will speak for themselves.

As a leader, disregard the insurmountable mountain before you when there are pebbles to get past first. Challenge yourself incessantly. You are the owner of your results and who you want to be. Nicco Annan said, "Good, better, best, never let it rest. While your good gets better, your better gets best." So don't be afraid to navigate the uncharted territory; all that is familiar to you now once wasn't.

Leadership Thoughts:

Weekly Charge:

Weekly Takeaways:

What I Need From You Is Understanding

Have you ever been going through a tough situation and began to vent to someone, only to be met with their own encounter or way to compare to the frustration you're expressing? If this happens once or twice, which could be a stretch, it could be tolerable, as the other person may be truly experiencing similar recourse. However, if this is habitual behavior, it leads to a lack of empathy and the perception of being a "Mr. Me Too." In Clipse's song, Mr. Me Too, they melodically record the lyrics, "Okay, everybody meet Mr. Me Too. I know what you thinkin', why I call you "Me Too?" 'Cause everythin' I say, I got you sayin', "Me too.""

Now, insert being a leader. Your team is looking for empathy, or in the words of Xscape, "What I Need From You Is Understanding." In demonstrating empathy, one is receptive and understanding of another's feelings or what they convey. Being a leader should be a safe space, within reason, not one where old war stories dominate the moment. This is where active listening is critical, and you get to learn more about your direct report and seek to form a bond.

When people come up with problems, asking if they want you to listen or your opinion is fine. Sometimes, people just need to express their thoughts out loud, and they tend to lead to their own solutions. There's no need to go from Clark Kent to Superman because someone expresses their thoughts or experiences.

It is alright just to be a listening ear, empathize, be sensitive to others, and provide understanding. As a leader, doing so will earn your team's and your peers' trust. Demonstrate being a leader amongst leaders and provide a different perspective in challenging the status quo. Provide some understanding.

Leadership Thoughts:

Weekly Charge:

Weekly Takeaways:

The Tightrope: Assertive versus Aggressive

The two words, assertive and aggressive, both indicate the need to do more and be more. There is a request to either earn or demand respect. On the one hand, assertiveness is viewed as being more inclusive and considerate of others. In contrast, aggressiveness can be perceived as disregarding others before oneself. Yet, when there's a need to go the extra mile professionally or even competitively in events, you hear statements of motivation for someone to assert themselves more or to be more aggressive.

While being assertive, one moves in confidence and force. In being aggressive, one confronts from a place of aggression via attitude or behavior. As aggressive has a negative connotation, the aggression can be directed towards a place of intrinsic motivation. Denial can fuel fire and alter a person's approach. Wrongdoings can also trigger this response, but they both can come from a place that exudes a competitive nature.

Nike has a campaign with the slogan "Winning Isn't For Everyone." At the ad's start, the question is posed, "Am I a bad person?" It then displays top athletes in their respective sports who have built themselves up and trained individually to be the best. The traits outlined can be perceived negatively, such as being strategic and selfish, yet it drives them to win and be the best. Here's the kicker—they are still respected as the best in their realm.

There's a fine line between the two, and it is the leader's responsibility to walk the tightrope so as not to be too much or too little of either. On one side, you can become overbearing to your team and peers with the desire to distance themselves. Conversely, you can come across as meek and not have a voice in the room. Walking the tightrope is personal to the leader in self-managing, and they ensure this balance is kept within the team's structure. Doing so will permit an environment of mutual respect.

Leadership Thoughts:

Weekly Charge:

Weekly Takeaways:

The Bar Has Been Set

When you hear the phrase, "The bar has been set," it indicates the goal has been established. In most cases, it is considered the standard one should strive to attain. It is the norm or average baseline and can be quantitative or qualitative. Qualitative standards are hard to measure definitively, but they set the expectation for being good. While standards are the proverbial notch of excellence, why not strive beyond the bar?

You should aim to be better each day than you were the day before. Hence, being a leader is no different. The goal is a mere standard that should be achievable. It is, in essence, the status quo. True leaders just don't want to be average; they should pour into others and seek to be better than average. They should strive not to meet the bar but exceed it.

As cliche as it sounds, you're in a battle with yourself. You are your only competition. Run with blinders on and pay no mind to the perceived flowers the next person receives. Your battle to surpass the bar and the accolades that come with it are only gaged on your unique leadership ability.

Yes, engagement surveys provide metrics to compare you with other leaders, but there's more to it. Is your team meeting performance metrics? Is the environment one of inclusivity? How are the dynamics and interactions of the team, both internally and externally? Is your team the "unicorn" that can come up with solutions to various challenges? These things allow you to meet the bar and clear it as if you were setting the World Record in a Track & Field event.

Leadership Thoughts:

Weekly Charge:

Weekly Takeaways:

You Give Me Butterflies

In his song, Butterflies, Michael Jackson sang about a person's anticipation and beauty when he said, "You give me butterflies inside." When you think about the stages of a butterfly, it starts from an egg, then to a caterpillar, next to a cocoon, transitions to a young butterfly, and finally, evolves into a beautiful butterfly. This growth process illustrates the process that takes place and the required time in between where there is no movement, just stillness. This is how we grow as people, more specifically, as leaders.

The journey of the butterfly is albeit a beautiful one, but there are periods of stagnancy where the beauty might not be seen. A social media post reads, "Butterflies rest when it rains because it damages their wings. It's okay to rest during the storms of life. You'll fly again when it's over." You will also experience some stagnation as a leader where you may not feel your best; moreover, you will soar, and your lowest moments will be used as character builders.

Society tends to push the perception that only the positive aspects can be celebrated, while social media puts a glaring fictional persona on it as well. Yet, it's in the losses of life and the even-keeled times where we really shine and evolve as a leader. Per A'ja Wilson, Dawn Staley says, "Never get too high with your highs. Never get too low with your lows." In this, it is the balance that creates the beauty that is embodied in your leadership.

As the butterfly grows, let it resonate with the work you put into perfecting your craft. The steps in between the egg and the butterfly are those that build great leaders. It's the soft skills, the experiences, and the traditional learning that aids in your growth. Jay-Z said in Most Kingz, "Everybody look at you strange, say you changed. Like you work that hard to stay the same."

Leadership Thoughts:

Weekly Charge:

Weekly Takeaways:

These Are My Reflections

In a period of reflection, you contemplate a situation or period of time that has occurred. It is your personal movie where there is happiness, sadness, opportunities, transition, growth, and triumph. There are multiple climaxes and plot twists. Nonetheless, YOUR story shapes who you are as a person. These experiences help you decide how you want to lead.

Margaret J. Wheatley says, "Without reflection, we go blindly on our way, creating more unintended consequences, and failing to achieve anything useful." Course correction is necessary along the journey; the only way to do so is to evaluate your path. Others will provide their perception of you as a person and leader. This will be their opinion based on a moment, good or bad, or several moments where your ability is analyzed. However, I've heard in various facets that opinions are like buttholes, and everyone has one. It is up to you to filter through what applies; besides that, it has no relevance to aid in your development.

As you reflect, it is not intended for you to stay there. It is merely the review of the test and how you performed. How you react to the challenges and opportunities dictates your performance on the next one. This is the strength of leaders in not always getting it right but navigating the path to do better in the future. Leaving the past behind allows you to better focus on and receive your opportunities for the future. The idea is to stop living out the definition of insanity.

Reflections are meant for growth and improvement. When you work to enhance yourself as a leader, ensure you create an atmosphere that enables others to thrive and desire to be around you and your team. As you reflect through the stages of your life, you might come out of this period with things looking different. Guess what? That's okay! B. Simone stated, "Highest level of success is not financial; it's fulfillment." Seek what fills and pours into you. Drop the extra baggage you've been carrying from the past; it'll make the trip much easier.

Leadership Thoughts:

Weekly Charge:

Weekly Takeaways:

About Janelle A. Jordan, DBA

Janelle Jordan was born in the Bronx, New York, and raised in Orangeburg, South Carolina. She is the daughter of Sandra Jordan and Reverend Andrew (late Shirley) Jordan. Janelle is the youngest of three girls from this union. Her older siblings are Anjelica Jordan-English and Janese Jordan. Janelle is the proud aunt of five nieces and nephews she considers her own: Imani Williams, Jamari Williams, Javon Williams, Amaris English, and Arielle English. Also, a brother-in-law, Joel English.

After graduating from Orangeburg Wilkinson High School as an honor student and student-athlete, Janelle was enrolled at North Carolina A&T State University. She graduated Magna Cum Laude with a Bachelor of Science Degree in Electrical Engineering. She later earned her Master of Business Administration Degree in General Management from Troy University and her Doctor of Business Administration Degree in Leadership from Liberty University.

Janelle has almost twenty years of experience, primarily in a corporate manufacturing environment, working in various locations and capacities, in addition to having entrepreneurial experience. Most of her professional career has been in management, where she has mentored and developed talent within organizational structures. Janelle is the Co-owner of CoJa Group, LLC, which rents commercial property, and the Owner of E.G.O. Leadership Consultants, LLC, where she is a Leadership Consultant and Speaker. Moreover, she is the author of *Still Not Enough: Minority Millennials in the Workforce.*

Outside of professional experiences, she has served as an Assistant Coach for Varsity Girls' Basketball at Orangeburg Wilkinson High School. While there and beyond, Janelle has mentored several young ladies outside the facets of basketball toward achieving their personal and professional endeavors. Janelle is also a member of Delta Sigma Theta Sorority, Incorporated.

FRESH INK GROUP

Independent Multi-media Publisher

Fresh Ink Group / Push Pull Press

Voice of Indie / GeezWriter

Hardcovers

Softcovers

All Ebook Formats

Audiobooks

Podcasts

Worldwide Distribution

Indie Author Services

Book Development, Editing, Proofing

Graphic/Cover Design

Video/Trailer Production

Website Creation

Social Media Marketing

Writing Contests

Writers' Blogs

Authors

Editors

Artists

Experts

Professionals

FreshInkGroup.com

info@FreshInkGroup.com

X: @FreshInkGroup

Facebook.com/FreshInkGroup

LinkedIn: Fresh Ink Group

Instagram: @FreshInkGroup and @FIGPublishing

Fresh Ink Group

FreshInkGroup.com

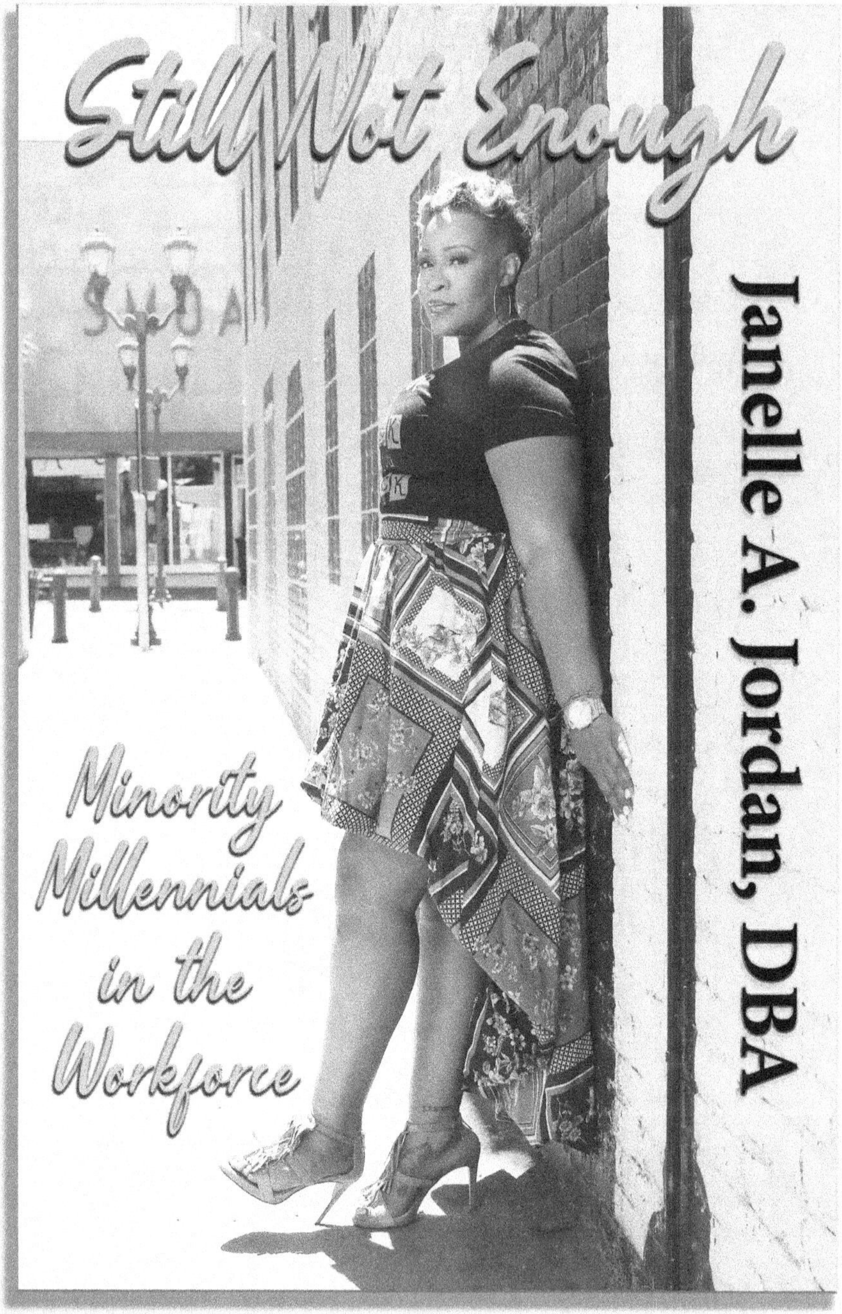

Still Not Enough examines the plight of minority Millennials in the workforce. Janelle details her own perspective-molding cultural upbringings along with professional encounters hindered by others' preconceived notions and unconscious biases. She shares examples that are relatable to many with similar experiences. The scars from every denial fuel the desire for each minority Millennial to do more. This book also guides leaders managing today's DE&I employees. Norms are evolving, and organizations must adapt or be left behind. Still Not Enough brings transparency to the challenges of today's younger and more-inclusive workforce.

Jacketed Hardcover
Softcover • All Ebooks

Fresh Ink Group
FreshInkGroup.com

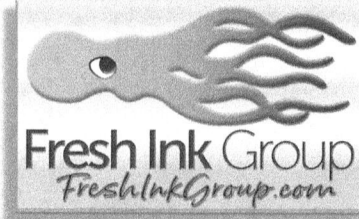

www.ingramcontent.com/pod-product-compliance
Lightning Source LLC
Chambersburg PA
CBHW081000120626
46546CB00010B/2978